Cool Hotels
Africa/Middle East

teNeues

Editor:	Martin Nicholas Kunz
Editorial coordination:	Patricia Massó
Editorial assistance:	Michelle Galindo, Susanne Olbrich, Nicole Rankers
Introduction:	Camilla Péus (travel & design editor, Hamburg, Germany)
Expert advise:	Anke Schaffelhuber and Conservation Corporation Africa (CCA)
Translations:	SAW Communications, Dr. Sabine A. Werner, Mainz
	Dr. Suzanne Kirkbright (English), Céline Verschelde (French),
	Maider Olarra (Spanish), Paola Lonardi (Italian)
Layout:	Michelle Galindo
Imaging & Pre-press:	Susanne Olbrich, Nicole Rankers
Maps:	Jan Hausberg
Produced by	fusion publishing GmbH, Stuttgart . Los Angeles
	www.fusion-publishing.com

Published by teNeues Publishing Group

teNeues Publishing Company
16 West 22nd Street, New York, NY 10010, USA
Tel.: 001-212-627-9090, Fax: 001-212-627-9511

teNeues Book Division
Kaistraße 18, 40221 Düsseldorf, Germany
Tel.: 0049-(0)211-994597-0, Fax: 0049-(0)211-994597-40

teNeues Publishing UK Ltd.
P.O. Box 402, West Byfleet, KT14 7ZF, Great Britain
Tel.: 0044-1932-403509, Fax: 0044-1932-403514

teNeues France S.A.R.L.
4, rue de Valence, 75005 Paris, France
Tel.: 0033-1-55766205, Fax: 0033-1-55766419

teNeues Iberica S.L.
Pso. Juan de la Encina, 2-48, Urb. Club de Campo
28700 S.S.R.R., Madrid, Spain
Tel./Fax: 0034-91-6595876

www.teneues.com

ISBN-10:	3-8327-9051-9
ISBN-13:	978-3-8327-9051-6

© 2005 teNeues Verlag GmbH + Co. KG, Kempen

Printed in Italy

Bibliographic information published by Die Deutsche
Bibliothek. Die Deutsche Bibliothek lists this publication
in the Deutsche Nationalbibliografie; detailed bibliographic
data is available in the Internet at http://dnb.ddb.de

Contents

South Africa

Introduction

The Victoria Falls rush to the depths in the distance, the Zambezi River flows right in front of the chalet terraces, bathing in the bathtub with lions' feet you can hear the sounds of the hippopotamus and in the evening, guests play croquet by candlelight on the hotel's English lawn. This description could fit an exclusive luxury resort, but it applies to a small hotel with a high standard of design and comfort: The River Club in Zambia. More and more of these hotel oases are being created in the most unusual locations in the middle of unspoiled nature and over the entire continent.

Another insider tip that avoids mass tourism is the Kaya Mawa Lodge in Malawi: its unique location on a crystal clear lake makes the hotel one of Africa's most relaxing destinations. Even in Mozambique, in Benguerra Lodge, travelers today can experience the wild vegetation and kilometer-long stretches of white sandy beaches, because meanwhile a democratic government has been installed in this country that was once ransacked by civil war. These surprising examples show that even in countries where tourism is still in its early stages, there are hotels out there whose owners have created a totally personal ambiance with lots of love of detail.

Hotels featuring in this book that also have unique concepts are located in the popular tourist destinations of South Africa, Namibia, Tanzania and the Sultanate of Oman. An exception among South Africa's hotels is The Outpost in the Kruger National Park: in the modern bungalows,

which are reminiscent of buildings by the architect Richard Neutra, floor-to-ceiling glass sliding doors open out onto nature. In Namibia, the Goche Ganas Hotel offers wilderness and fitness up on a high plateau: travelers here can treat themselves to massages in a grotto sauna and an indoor swimming pool. The Hatari Lodge in Tanzania is also extravagant: the ten suites are decorated in retro look; the walls are painted with bright Op Art designs. And in The Chedi in Muscat, oriental ornamentation was interpreted in minimalist style.

As different as they are, these hotels have one thing in common: they are all clearly distinguished from standard hotel chains and holiday clubs. Mostly, they are small facilities with a dozen pavilions or huts, which harmonize with the landscape, either being built around cliffs or else they are so well camouflaged in the wetlands of the world famous Okavango Delta that elephants trot right up to the front door.

Camilla Péus

Einleitung

In der Ferne rauschen die Viktoriafälle in die Tiefe, vor den Terrassen der Chalets fließt der Sambesi, beim Bad in der löwenfüßigen Wanne hört man die Laute der Flusspferde und abends spielen Gäste bei Kerzenschein Krocket auf dem englischen Rasen des Hotels. Diese Beschreibung könnte auf ein exklusives Luxus-Resort passen, doch gemeint ist ein kleines Hotel mit hohem Anspruch an Design und Komfort: The River Club in Sambia. Immer mehr solcher Hotel-Oasen entstehen an den ungewöhnlichsten Orten inmitten ursprünglicher Natur auf dem gesamten Kontinent.

Ein anderer Geheimtipp abseits des Massentourismus ist die Kaya Mawa Lodge in Malawi: Ihre einzigartige Lage an einem kristallklaren See macht das Hotel zu einem der erholsamsten Ziele Afrikas. Sogar in Mosambik, in der Benguerra Lodge, können Reisende heute die wilde Vegetation und kilometerlange weiße Sandstrände erleben, denn in dem einst von Bürgerkriegen gebeutelten Land hat sich inzwischen eine demokratische Regierung etabliert. Diese überraschenden Beispiele zeigen, dass selbst in Ländern, in denen der Tourismus noch in den Kinderschuhen steckt, Hotels zu finden sind, deren Inhaber mit Liebe zum Detail ein ganz persönliches Ambiente geschaffen haben.

Einmalige Konzepte präsentieren auch die in diesem Buch vorgestellten Hotels in den beliebten Reiseländern Südafrika, Namibia, Tansania und dem Sultanat Oman. Eine Ausnahmestellung unter Südafrikas Hotels nimmt The Outpost im Kruger-Nationalpark ein: In den modernen Bungalows, die an Bauten des Architekten Richard Neutra erinnern,

öffnen sich raumhohe Glasschiebetüren zur Natur. In Namibia bietet das Goche Ganas Hotel Wildnis und Wellness auf einem Hochplateau: Reisende können sich dort in einer Grottensauna und einem Hallenbad mit Massagen verwöhnen lassen. Extravagant ist auch die Hatari Lodge in Tansania: Die zehn Suiten sind im Retro-Look dekoriert, die Wände mit bunten Op-Art-Mustern bemalt. Und im The Chedi in Muskat wurde orientalische Ornamentik minimalistisch interpretiert.

So unterschiedlich sie auch sind, eines haben diese Hotels gemeinsam: Sie alle heben sich deutlich von standardisierten Ketten und Ferienclubs ab. Es sind meist kleine Anlagen mit einem Dutzend Pavillons oder Hütten, die sich harmonisch in die Landschaft einfügen, um Felsen herumgebaut sind oder so gut getarnt in den Feuchtwiesen des weltberühmten Okavangodeltas liegen, dass Elefanten bis vor die Haustür traben.

Camilla Péus

Introduction

Le bruit des chutes Victoria est perceptible au lointain, le Zambèze coule devant les terrasses des chalets, on reconnaît le son des hippopotames lorsque l'on prend son bain dans une baignoire aux pieds de lion et le soir, à la lumière de la bougie, les hôtes jouent au croquet sur la pelouse anglaise de l'hôtel. Cette description pourrait être celle d'un resort de luxe exclusif, mais il s'agit bien d'un petit hôtel accordant une importance capitale au design et au confort : The River Club en Zambie. De plus en plus d'oasis de ce type apparaissent sur tout le continent aux endroits les plus inhabituels, au milieu de la nature originelle.

Le Kaya Mawa Lodge, situé à Malawi, loin du tourisme de masse, est un autre conseil d'initiés : sa situation unique au bord d'un lac limpide fait de l'hôtel l'une des destinations les plus reposantes de toute l'Afrique. Même au Mozambique, dans le Benguerra Lodge, les touristes peuvent aujourd'hui découvrir la végétation sauvage et des kilomètres de plages de sable blanc depuis qu'un gouvernement démocratique s'est imposé dans ce pays autrefois malmené par les guerres civiles. Ces exemples surprenants montrent que, même dans des pays où le tourisme est encore dans ses jeunes années, on peut trouver des hôtels où les propriétaires ont créé une ambiance personnelle en apportant beaucoup de soin au détail.

Les hôtels se trouvant dans des lieux touristiques comme l'Afrique du Sud, la Namibie, la Tanzanie et le sultanat Oman et qui sont présentés dans cet ouvrage offrent également des concepts uniques. Parmi

les hôtels d'Afrique du Sud, The Outpost, situé dans le parc national Kruger, jouit d'un site d'exception : dans les bungalows modernes rappelant les constructions de l'architecte Richard Neutra, des baies vitrées coulissantes de la hauteur de la pièce s'ouvrent sur la nature. En Namibie, le Goche Ganas Hotel offre région déserte et bien-être sur un plateau surélevé : là-bas, les touristes peuvent se faire dorloter avec des massages dans un sauna aménagé dans une grotte et une piscine couverte. Le Hatari Lodge, en Tanzanie, est tout aussi extravagant : les dix suites sont décorées en look rétro, les murs peints de motifs Op-Art colorés. The Chedi, à Muscat, a mis l'accent sur une ornementation orientale minimaliste.

Tous différents, ces hôtels ont un point commun : ils se distinguent nettement des chaînes et des clubs de vacances standards. Ce sont la plupart du temps des petites installations comprenant une douzaine de pavillons ou de cabanes qui se fondent avec harmonie dans le paysage, qui entourent des rochers ou qui sont si bien camouflées dans les prés humides du célèbre delta de l'Okavango que les éléphants s'aventurent jusqu'à la porte d'entrée.

Camilla Péus

Introducción

A lo lejos se oye el murmullo de las cataratas Victoria, ante las terrazas de los chalets fluye el río Zambeze, desde la bañera, con patas en forma de pezuña de león, se puede escuchar a los hipopótamos, y por las noches los huéspedes se divierten jugando al croquet a la luz de las velas en el césped inglés del hotel. Si bien ésta podría ser la descripción de un exclusivo complejo de lujo, estamos hablando de un pequeño hotel capaz de satisfacer altas exigencias de diseño y confort: The River Club de Zambia. Cada vez nacen más oasis hoteleros de este tipo en los lugares más insospechados de todo el continente, en plena naturaleza virgen.

Otro verdadero hallazgo lejano al turismo de masas es Kaya Mawa Lodge de Malawi: su ubicación de carácter único a orillas de un lago cristalino convierte al hotel en uno de los destinos más relajantes de África. Incluso en Mozambique, en Benguerra Lodge, los viajeros pueden disfrutar de la vegetación salvaje y de playas blancas kilométricas, ya que este país, que en su día fue sacudido por las guerras civiles, tiene un gobierno democrático. Estos asombrosos ejemplos son muestra de que, incluso en los países en los que el turismo aún está en su fase inicial, se pueden encontrar hoteles cuyos propietarios han creado un ambiente muy personal con cada uno de sus detalles.

Los hoteles recogidos en este libro también presentan conceptos únicos que pueden disfrutarse en destinos apreciados por el turismo como Sudáfrica, Namibia, Tanzania y la sultanía de Omán. Entre los

hoteles sudafricanos, The Outpost situado en el parque nacional Kruger es algo diferente: en los modernos bungalows que recuerdan a las construcciones del arquitecto Richard Neutra, las ventanas correderas hasta el techo se abren hacia la naturaleza. En Namibia, Goche Ganas Hotel ofrece una combinación de fauna y wellness en una meseta: allí, los viajeros pueden dejarse mimar con masajes en una gruta-sauna y una piscina cubierta. Hatari Lodge de Tanzania encandila con un toque extravagante: sus diez suits están decoradas con un estilo retro, las paredes pintadas con coloridos motivos op art. Y en The Chedi de Muskat la ornamentación oriental ha sido interpretada de forma minimalista.

A pesar de la diversidad de estos hoteles, todos tienen algo en común: se distancian claramente de las cadenas estandarizadas y de los clubs vacacionales. Suelen ser pequeñas instalaciones con una docena de edificios o casetas que armonizan con el paisaje, que se han construido entorno a peñas o que reposan en las praderas húmedas del famoso delta del Okavango de forma tan camuflada que hasta los elefantes se acercan a tocar a la puerta.

Camilla Péus

Introduzione

Il tuffo scrosciante nel vuoto delle Cascate Vittoria si sente in lontananza, il fiume Zambesi scorre direttamente davanti al terrazzo degli chalet, i versi degli ippopotami fanno da sottofondo al bagno rilassante nella vasca dai piedini a ricciolo e gli ospiti la sera giocano a croquet a lume di candela sul prato inglese. No, non è la descrizione di un esclusivo resort di lusso bensì quella di un hotel che non rinuncia a design e comfort nonostante le dimensioni contenute: The River Club in Zambia. In tutto il continente sono sempre più numerose le oasi come questa che nascono in luoghi insoliti, immerse nella natura incontaminata.

Un altro suggerimento prezioso per chi è alla ricerca di luoghi lontani dal turismo di massa è il Kaya Mawa Lodge nel Malawi: l'incomparabile tranquillità del luogo, che si rispecchia nelle acque cristalline del lago, rende questo resort una meta unica per vacanze tutto riposo nel continente africano. Oggi perfino in Mozambico, nel Benguerra Lodge, i turisti possono godersi la vegetazione selvaggia e le spiagge bianche che si estendono per interi chilometri. Ciò è reso possibile dagli effetti positivi del governo democratico insediatosi nel paese un tempo martoriato dalle guerre civili. Questi esempi sorprendenti dimostrano che perfino in paesi in cui il turismo rappresenta un fenomeno del tutto nuovo è possibile trovare degli hotel cui i proprietari e il loro amore per il dettaglio hanno saputo infondere una nota tutta personale.

Le straordinarie formule di progettazione degli hotel presentati in questo libro hanno come sfondo mete molto amate dai turisti: Sudafrica,

Namibia, Tanzania e il Sultanato dell'Oman. Fra gli hotel del Sudafrica spicca per originalità l'Outpost, ubicato nel Parco Kruger: i moderni bungalow, che ricordano lo stile dell'architetto Richard Neutra, hanno grandi porte scorrevoli vetrate a tutta altezza che aprendosi direttamente sul paesaggio sembrano compenetrare la natura. In Namibia il Goche Ganas Hotel, costruito su un altopiano, permette di conciliare vita primitiva e benessere. I turisti possono farsi coccolare con dei massaggi nella sauna in grotta e nella piscina coperta. Un resort molto originale è anche l'Hatari Lodge in Tanzania, composto di dieci suite in stile retrò look dalle pareti con decorazioni colorate Op'Art. All'hotel The Chedi a Muskat l'ornamentazione orientale viene presentata nella sua interpretazione in chiave minimalista.

Per quanto diversi l'uno dall'altro, gli hotel hanno un unico comune denominatore: si differenziano nettamente dalle catene alberghiere standardizzate e dai soliti villaggi vacanze. Sono perlopiù strutture dalle dimensioni contenute, costituite da circa una decina di capanne o di pavillon che ben si armonizzano con la natura circostante, costruiti attorno a massi rocciosi o così ben nascosti nelle radure del delta del fiume Okovango che non ci sarebbe nulla da stupirsi se un elefante, trotterellando, si spingesse fin sulla soglia.

Camilla Péus

Northern
Africa

Morocco

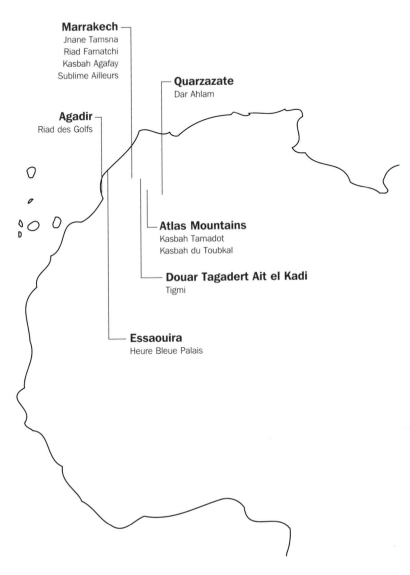

Marrakech
Jnane Tamsna
Riad Farnatchi
Kasbah Agafay
Sublime Ailleurs

Quarzazate
Dar Ahlam

Agadir
Riad des Golfs

Atlas Mountains
Kasbah Tamadot
Kasbah du Toubkal

Douar Tagadert Ait el Kadi
Tigmi

Essaouira
Heure Bleue Palais

Riad des Golfs

Address:	Ben Sergao, Les golfs
	80 000 Agadir, Morocco
Phone:	+212 44 43 19 00
Fax:	+212 44 43 17 86
Website:	www.riadomaroc.com
e-mail:	riadomaroc@menara.ma
Located:	near by the center of Agadir, in an eucalyptus forest close to the Royal Palace
Style:	Moorish, elegant
Special features:	3 dining rooms, terraces, numerous gardens, hammam, swimming pool
Rooms:	8 junior suites
Opening date:	2003
Architecture / Design:	Paule et Bernard Brilhault

Kasbah Tamadot

Address: Atlas Mountains, Morocco
Phone: +44 20 8600 0430
Fax: +44 20 8600 0431

Website: www.virgin.com/limitededition
e-mail: enquiries@limitededition.virgin.co.uk

Located: in the foothills of the Atlas Mountains,
a 45 minutes drive south of Marrakech
Style: traditional Moroccan meets contemporary chic
Special features: hammam, gym, sauna, library, restaurant, tennis
courts, rooftop seating area, indoor & outdoor
pools
Rooms: 18 rooms, including suites. The hotel can be
hired exclusively

Opening date: 2005

Architecture / Design: Virgin

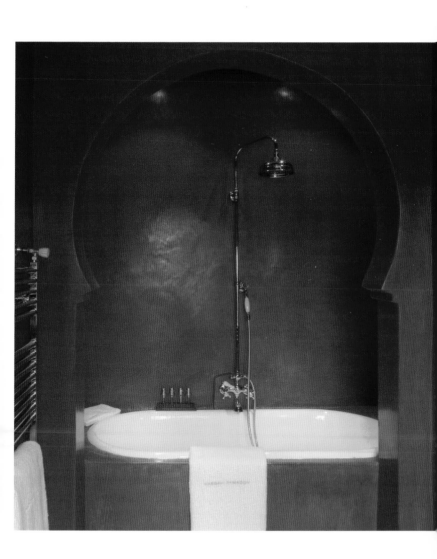

Kasbah du Toubkal

Address: Atlas Mountains, Morocco
Phone: +212 44 48 56 11
Fax: +212 44 48 56 36

Website: www.kasbahdutoubkal.com
e-mail: kasbah@discover.ltd.uk

Located: 60 km from Marrakech, at the foot of
Jbel Toubkal—the highest peak in
North Africa
Style: traditional Moroccan
Special features: conference facilities, roof top terrace
Rooms: 11 rooms, 3 Berber saloons

Opening date: 1995

Architecture / Design: Kasbah du Toubkal team

Tigmi

Address:	Km 24 Route d'Amizmiz
	Douar Tagadert Ait el Kadi, Morocco
Phone:	+44 1380 828 533
Fax:	+44 1380 828 630
Website:	www.tigmi.com
e-mail:	tigmi@realmorocco.com
Located:	on the brow of Tagadert, in a Berber hamlet in the Haouz Plain, 15 miles from the medieval city of Marrakech
Style:	organic, traditional
Special features:	restaurant, hammam, TV room
Rooms:	8 suites
Opening date:	2002
Architecture / Design:	Max Lawrence

Heure Bleue Palais

Address:	2 Rue Ibn Batouta
	44 000 Essaouira, Morocco
Phone:	+212 44 78 34 34
Fax:	+212 44 47 42 22
Website:	www.riadsmorocco.com
e-mail:	reservations@riadsmorocco.com
Located:	next to the Bab Marrakech in the Medina of Essaouira
Style:	African colonial, elegant
Special features:	rooftop terrace, rooftop swimming pool and bar, restaurant, screening room, Turkish baths, spa
Rooms:	16 rooms and 19 suites
Opening date:	2004
rchitecture / Design:	Karl Fournier and Olivier Marty from Studio KO

Jnane Tamsna

Address:	Douar Abiad, Circuit de la Palmeraie La Palmeraie Marrakech, Morocco
Phone:	+212 44 32 94 23
Fax:	+212 44 32 98 84
Website:	www.jnanetamsna.com
e-mail:	meryanne@jnanetamsna.com
Located:	15 minutes drive from Marrakech city center
Style:	Moorish country hacienda
Special features:	3 pools and one clay surface, tennis court, 6 acres of gardens, among them organic herbs and vegetable gardens
Rooms:	country guesthouse with 17 rooms
Opening date:	2001
Architecture / Design:	Meryanne Loum-Martin

Riad Farnatchi

Address:	2 Derb el Farnatchi
	40 000 Marrakech Medina, Morocco
Phone:	+212 44 38 49 10
Fax:	+212 44 38 49 13
Website:	www.riadfarnatchi.com
e-mail:	Info@riadfarnatchi.com
Located:	in the heart of the oldest part of Marrakech
Style:	Moroccan fusion
Special features:	roof garden with barbecue, hammam
Rooms:	8 suites
Opening date:	2004
Architecture / Design:	Jonathan Wix from Riad Farnatchi
	Carlos Bancolini from Khamsa

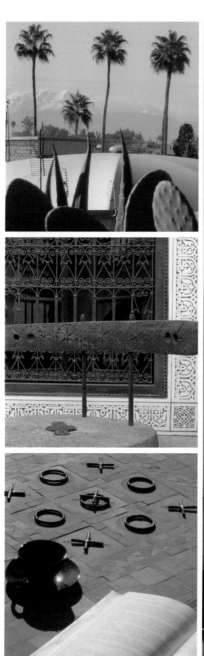

Kasbah Agafay

Address:	Route de Guemassa
	40 000 Marrakech, Morocco
Phone:	+212 44 36 86 00
Fax:	+212 44 42 09 70
Website:	www.kasbahagafay.com
e-mail:	info@kasbahagafay.com
Located:	in the Medina of Marrakech
Style:	traditional
Special features:	cookery school
Rooms:	9 rooms, 6 suites and 5 luxury suites
Opening date:	Reopened 2001
Architecture / Design:	Abel Damoussi
	Quintin Willbaux

Sublime Ailleurs

Address:	B.P. 2309
	40 000 Marrakech, Morocco
Phone:	+212 44 32 96 44/46
Fax:	+212 44 32 96 45
Website:	www.sublimeailleurs.com
e-mail:	sublimeailleurs@wanadoo.net.ma
Located:	in the heart of the Marrakech palm grove
Style:	traditional Moroccan
Special features:	spa, medical treatments, beauty care, organic garden
Rooms:	8 rooms
Opening date:	2001
Architecture / Design:	Marie-Claude Azzouzi

Dar Ahlam

Address:	Casbah Madihi, Palmeraie de Skoura
	Quarzazate, Morocco
Phone:	+212 44 85 22 39
Fax:	+212 44 85 22 39
Website:	www.darahlam.com
e-mail:	darahlam@leverderideau.fr
Located:	30 minutes from the Ouarzazate
	international airport
Style:	elegant, traditional
Special features:	hammam, drawing rooms
Rooms:	3 villas
Opening date:	2003
Architecture / Design:	Thierry Teyssier

Near & Middle East

**Lebanon
Syria
United Arab Emirates
Oman**

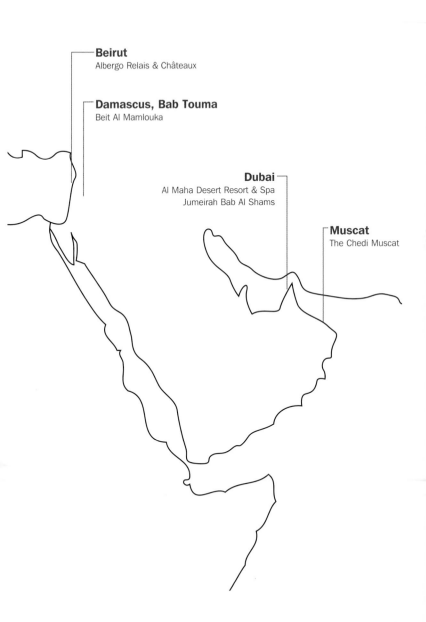

Beirut
Albergo Relais & Châteaux

Damascus, Bab Touma
Beit Al Mamlouka

Dubai
Al Maha Desert Resort & Spa
Jumeirah Bab Al Shams

Muscat
The Chedi Muscat

Albergo Relais & Châteaux

Address:	137, Abdel Wahab El Inglizi Street
	Beirut, Lebanon
Phone:	+961 1 33 97 97
Fax:	+961 1 33 99 99
Website:	www.albergobeirut.com
e-mail:	albergo@relaischateaux.com
Located:	in the heart of old Eastern Beirut,
	5 km from Beirut International Airport
Style:	luxury, elegant, ageless
Special features:	2 restaurants, terrace
Rooms:	33 suites
Opening date:	1998
Architecture / Design:	Jacques Garcia, Tarfa Salam

Albergo Relais & Châteaux | **95**

Beit Al Mamlouka

Address:	Quaimarieh Street, near Hammam Bakri, Bab Touma, Damascus, Syria
Phone:	+963 11 543 0445
Fax:	+963 11 541 7248
Website:	www.almamlouka.com
e-mail:	almamlouka@mail.sy
Located:	in the heart of the old city, about 2 minutes walk from Bab Touma and 8 minutes from Omayyad Mosque and the old Souk
Style:	historical and elegant
Special features:	18th and 19th century ceilings with frescoes on the wall, lounge and dining area in an old reconverted stable
Rooms:	8 rooms including 4 suites
Opening date:	2005
Architecture / Design:	Simone Kosremelli

Al Maha Desert Resort & Spa

Dubai | United Arab Emirates

Address:	Dubai, United Arab Emirates
Phone:	+971 4 303 4222
Fax:	+971 4 343 9696
Website:	www.al-maha.com
e-mail:	almaha@emirates.com
Located:	set within a 225 square kilometer desert conservation reserve, 45 km from the city of Dubai
Style:	traditional Bedouin encampment
Special features:	Jamilah Spa & Leisure Center, swimming pool, conference center
Rooms:	43 suites
Opening date:	1999
Architecture / Design:	Schuster Pechthold + Partners, Wrenn Associates, Rashid Taqui

Jumeirah Bab Al Shams

Address:	Dubai, United Arab Emirates
Phone:	+971 4 832 6699
Fax:	+971 4 832 6698
Website:	www.jumeirah.com
e-mail:	info@jumeirah.com
Located:	close by the Endurance Village, 45 minutes from Dubai International Airport
Style:	rustic Arabic, traditional Gulf décor
Special features:	open-air Arabic desert restaurant, 2 restaurants, 3 bars and lounges, spa, gym, boutique, prayer room
Rooms:	115 rooms and suites
Opening date:	2004
Architecture / Design:	Keith Gavin, Godwin Austen Johnson Karen Wilhelmm, Mirage Mille

The Chedi Muscat

Address:	North Ghubra 232, Way No. 3215, Street No. 46 Muscat, Oman
Phone:	+968 24 52 44 00
Fax:	+968 24 49 34 85
Website:	www.ghmhotels.com
e-mail:	chedimuscat@ghmhotels.com
Located:	on the stunning Boushar beachfront in Oman
Style:	elegant, stylish, traditional
Special features:	1 restaurant, 2 cabanas, lobby lounge, club lounge, private beach, spa, library, boutique, gallery, conference facilities
Rooms:	151 rooms and suites
Opening date:	2002
Architecture / Design:	Jean-Michael Gathy Yasuhiro Koichi

Indian Ocean
Central &
Eastern Africa

Mauritius
Kenya
Tanzania
Malawi
Zambia
Zimbabwe

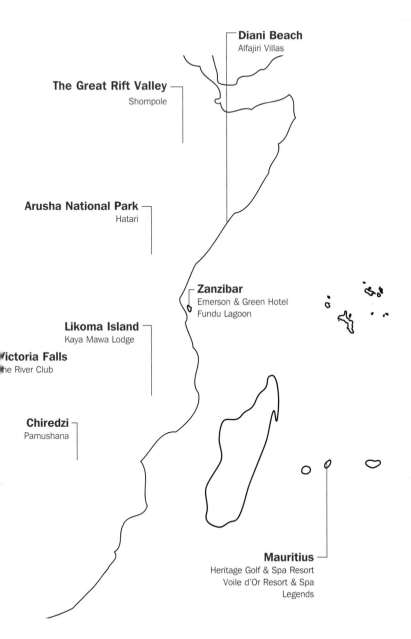

Diani Beach
Alfajiri Villas

The Great Rift Valley
Shompole

Arusha National Park
Hatari

Zanzibar
Emerson & Green Hotel
Fundu Lagoon

Likoma Island
Kaya Mawa Lodge

Victoria Falls
The River Club

Chiredzi
Pamushana

Mauritius
Heritage Golf & Spa Resort
Voile d'Or Resort & Spa
Legends

Heritage Golf & Spa Resort

Address:	Bel Ombre, Mauritius
Phone:	+230 266 9700
Fax:	+230 266 9797
Website:	www.veranda-resorts.com
e-mail:	veranda@veranda-resorts.com
Located:	on the South Coast near Bel Ombre, 50 minutes to the airport, 75 minutes to the capital Port Louis
Style:	elegant, classical, contemporary
Special features:	5 restaurants, 3 bars, 18 hole golf course, spa, conference room, business center, sport & water sport facilities, entertainment
Rooms:	154 deluxe rooms, 5 suites, 1 villa
Opening date:	2004
Architecture / Design:	Jean Marc Eynaud VK Design, Virginie Koenig

Voile d'Or Resort & Spa

Address:	Allée des Cocotiers
	Bel Ombre, Mauritius
Phone:	+230 623 50 00
Fax:	+230 623 50 01
Website:	www.voiledor.com
e-mail:	info@voiledor.com
Located:	on a 500 meter stretch of beach at Bel Ombre on the South West coast
Style:	elegant, classic, luxury
Special features:	3 restaurants, 4 bars, club area, music room, spa, library, business center, sport & water sport facilities, bowling center, 3 boutiques, deli shop
Rooms:	181 rooms, club rooms and suites
Opening date:	2004
Architecture / Design:	Jean Francois Koenig, Koenig Associates Architects
	Jean Pier D'Argent, J P D'Argent Interior Design

Legends

Address:	Pointe Réjane, Grand Gaube, Mauritius
Phone:	+230 204 9191
Fax:	+230 288 2828
Website:	www.naiade.com
e-mail:	legends@naiade.com
Located:	on northeast coast, near small village of Grand Gaube in isolated position on the beach
Style:	harmonizing, luxurious
Special features:	4 restaurants, beach bar and grill, bar, entertainment, cinema, boardroom, business center, deli shop, spa, gym, sport & water sport facilities
Rooms:	126 superior rooms, 46 deluxe rooms, 23 junior suites, 2 senior suites, 1 presidential villa
Opening date:	2002
Architecture / Design:	Jean François Adam
	Virginie Koenig

Shompole

Address:	P.O. Box 10665 Nairobi, Kenya (Reservations)
Phone:	+254 20 88 41 35
Fax:	+254 20 88 32 80
Website:	www.shompole.com
e-mail:	info@shompole.com
Located:	In the Great Rift Valley, 120 km south of Nairobi, on the edge of the Nguruman Escarpment
Style:	unique and artistically designed with natural materials
Special features:	main lounge and dining area, private cool-pools and lounges, activities
Rooms:	6 rooms, 2 suites
Opening date:	2001
Architecture / Design:	Anthony Russel, Neil Rocher, Elisabeth Warner

Alfajiri Villas

Address: Diana Beach, Kenya
Phone: +254 40 32 02 630
Fax: +254 40 32 02 218

Website: www.alfajirivillas.com
e-mail: reservation@alfajirivillas.com

Located: on the South Coast in Diani, one hour from Mombasa Airport
Style: bright and airy Caribbean style
Special features: inclusive of 15 staff, all food and drinks, massage, reflexology and 18 hole golf course
Rooms: a total of 12 rooms in the 3 villas

Opening date: Cliff Villa 2000, Garden and Beach Villa 2004

Architecture / Design: Marika Serafin

Hatari

Address:	Momella
	Arusha National Park, Tanzania
Phone:	+255 27 255 3456/7
Fax:	+255 27 255 3458
Website:	www.hatarilodge.com
e-mail:	marlies@theafricanembassy.com
Located:	on the foot of Mt. Meru, beyond Kilimandjaro at the northern edge of Arusha National Park
Style:	modern retro 60's and 70's style
Special features:	living and dining room, open fireplace, breakfast terrace, bar, library and wooden walkway for game viewing
Rooms:	8 rooms with their own private fireplace and terrace
Opening date:	2004
Architecture / Design:	Jörg & Marlies Gabriel

Emerson & Green Hotel

Address:	236 Hurumzi Street
	Zanzibar, Tanzania
Phone:	+255 747 42 32 66
Fax:	+255 747 42 92 66
Website:	www.emerson-green.com
e-mail:	emerson&green@zitec.org
Located:	in the heart of Stone Town
Style:	elegant, traditionally furnished
Special features:	Tower Top Restaurant, Kidude Café,
	Hurumzi Gallery boutique
Rooms:	16 rooms
Opening date:	1994
Architecture / Design:	Emerson Skeens & Thomas Green

Fundu Lagoon

Address:	Pemba Island, Zanzibar
	Tanzania
Phone:	+255 747 43 86 68
Fax:	+255 747 41 99 06
Website:	www.fundulagoon.com
e-mail:	fundu@africaonline.co.tz
Located:	on Pemba Island, the sister island to Zanzibar, on the southwestern side of the island. It is only accessible by boat.
Style:	natural, aboriginal
Special features:	restaurant, 2 bars, games and TV room, massage and treatment room, boutique
Rooms:	16 bungalows including 4 suites
Opening date:	2000
Architecture / Design:	Ellis Flyte

Kaya Mawa Lodge

Address:	P.O. Box 5219, Rivonia 2128 South Africa (Reservations)
Phone:	+27 11 807 1800
Fax:	+27 11 807 2110
Website:	www.wilderness-safaris.com
e-mail:	enquiry@wilderness.co.za
Located:	on the southern tip of Likoma Island, on the edge of a long beach bordered by two rocky promontories
Style:	traditional, elegant
Special features:	private honeymoon island, bar, dining room, rock pool
Rooms:	10 rooms
Opening date:	1997
Architecture / Design:	Will Sutton and Andrew Came

The River Club

Address:	P.O. Box 5219, Rivonia
	2128 South Africa (Reservations)
Phone:	+27 11 807 1800
Fax:	+27 11 807 2110
Website:	www.wilderness-safaris.com
e-mail:	enquiry@wilderness.co.za
Located:	on the Zambian side of the Zambezi River,
	18 km upstream from Victoria Falls
Style:	Edwardian
Special features:	library, drawing room, croquet lawn,
	card tables and board games, curio shop
Rooms:	10 chalets
Opening date:	1998
Architecture / Design:	Ivan Pantic, Peter Jones

Pamushana

Address:	Shop 37 Arundel Village
	Quorn Ave., Mount Pleasant
	Harare (Chiredzi), Zimbabwe
Phone:	+263 436 91 36
Fax:	+263 436 95 23
Website:	www.pamushana.com
e-mail:	mctsales@africaonline.co.zw
Located:	high on the edge of a rocky promontory overlooking a mountain backed lake
Style:	exotic, African
Special features:	cigar cave, gym, sauna, gift boutique, frescoed dining room
Rooms:	6 villas
Opening date:	1998
Architecture / Design:	Cecile Tilley & Boyd Ferguson

Southern Africa

Mozambique
Botswana
Namibia
South Africa

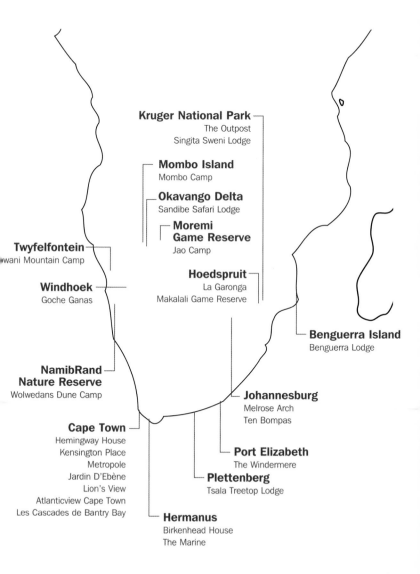

Kruger National Park
The Outpost
Singita Sweni Lodge

Mombo Island
Mombo Camp

Okavango Delta
Sandibe Safari Lodge

**Moremi
Game Reserve**
Jao Camp

Twyfelfontein
wani Mountain Camp

Windhoek
Goche Ganas

Hoedspruit
La Garonga
Makalali Game Reserve

Benguerra Island
Benguerra Lodge

**NamibRand
Nature Reserve**
Wolwedans Dune Camp

Johannesburg
Melrose Arch
Ten Bompas

Cape Town
Hemingway House
Kensington Place
Metropole
Jardin D'Ebène
Lion's View
Atlanticview Cape Town
Les Cascades de Bantry Bay

Port Elizabeth
The Windermere

Plettenberg
Tsala Treetop Lodge

Hermanus
Birkenhead House
The Marine

Benguerra Lodge

Address:	Benguerra Island Mozambique
Phone:	+271 14 52 06 41
Fax:	+271 14 52 14 96
Website:	www.benguerra.co.za
e-mail:	benguerra@icon.co.za
Located:	situated in the Bazaruto Archipelago of islands, o the southeastern border of Southern Africa.
Style:	East African with Arabian decor
Special features:	each chalet is no more than 20 meters from the beach
Rooms:	11 chalets, 2 honeymoon suites and 1 villa
Opening date:	2003
Architecture / Design:	Trevor Landrey

Mombo Camp

Address: P.O. Box 5219, Rivonia
2128 South Africa (Reservations)
Phone: +27 11 807 1800
Fax: +27 11 807 2110

Website: www.wilderness-safaris.com
e-mail: enquiry@wilderness.co.za

Located: on Mombo Island, adjoining the northern tip of
Chief's Island, within the Moremi Game Reserve
in the Okavango Delta in northern Botswana
Style: eco-architecture
Special features: bar, library
Rooms: 9 tents

Opening date: 2000

Architecture / Design: Silvio Rech & Lesley Carstens

Jao Camp

Address:	P.O. Box 5219, Rivonia 2128 South Africa (Reservations)
Phone:	+27 11 807 1800
Fax:	+27 11 807 2110
Website:	www.wilderness-safaris.com
e-mail:	enquiry@wilderness.co.za
Located:	on a remote large island, to the west of the Moremi Game Reserve in the heart of the Okavango Delta
Style:	eco-architecture
Special features:	pub, curio shop, library, campfire, massage salon
Rooms:	9 rooms
Opening date:	1999
Architecture / Design:	Sylvio Rech & Leslie Carstens

Sandibe Safari Lodge

Address:	Okavango Delta, Botswana
Phone:	+27 11 809 4300
Fax:	+27 11 809 4400
Website:	www.sandibe.com
e-mail:	reservations@ccafrica.com
Located:	in the southeastern Okavango Delta, 20 km east of Chief's Island, on the southern border of Moremi Game Reserve and within the Sandibe River system
Style:	organic, African-inspired
Special features:	open fireplace, swimming pool in the forest, bush dinners, library, gift shop
Rooms:	8 safari cottages
Opening date:	1998
Architecture / Design:	Chris Brown

Wolwedans Dune Camp

Address:	NamibRand Nature Reserve, Namibia
Phone:	+264 61 230 616
Fax:	+264 61 220 102
Website:	www.wolwedans.com
e-mail:	info@wolwedans.com.na
Located:	in the heart of NamibRand Nature Reserve, 60 km south of Sossusvlei
Style:	rustic-safari
Special features:	on the edge of a 250 meter high dune, intimate atmosphere, maximum of 12 guests
Rooms:	6 tents on wooden platforms, furnished with standard beds, veranda, private bathroom
Opening date:	1994
Architecture / Design:	Stephan Brückner

Mowani Mountain Camp

Address:	Twyfelfontein, Namibia
Phone:	+264 61 232 009
Fax:	+264 61 222 574
Website:	www.mowani.com
e-mail:	mowani@visionsofafrica.com.na
Located:	between the Ugab and Huab rivers, in Twyfelfontein Conservancy amongst huge boulders
Style:	East-African
Special features:	restaurant, lounge, bar, pool
Rooms:	12 tents on wooden platforms with veranda, all with en suite facilities. 1 luxury room, 1 suite
Opening date:	2000
Architecture / Design:	André Louw

Goche Ganas

Address: P.O. Box 40770
Windhoek, Namibia
Phone: +264 61 22 49 09
Fax: +264 61 22 49 24

Website: www.gocheganas.com
e-mail: info@gocheganas.com

Located: 29 km southeast from Windhoek, on a
hilltop overlooking a spectacular landscape
Style: elegant African
Special features: cave sauna, fitness and gym facilities, spa
with 10 treatment rooms
Rooms: 1 crown suite, 5 superior suites, 10 suites

Opening date: 2004

Architecture / Design: Ingo & Udo Stritter, Andrew Horne (Architecture)
Ingo, Sabine & Annemarie Stritter,
Sonja Kipping (Interior Design)

Hemingway House

Address: No. 1 & 2 Lodge Street, Oranjezicht
Cape Town, 8001 South Africa
Phone: +27 21 461 1857
Fax: +27 21 461 1857

Website: www.hemingwayhouse.co.za
e-mail: info@hemingwayhouse.co.za

Located: off Upper Orange Street in Oranjezicht
Style: afro-colonial chic, soul & spirit within spaces
Special features: open lounge with fireplace, its size makes you
feel like you are in your own house
Rooms: 2 separate buildings: Hemingway House has 4
rooms and the Lodge 3 rooms

Opening date: 2000 (The House) 2005 (The Lodge)

Architecture / Design: Josephine Hemingway

Kensington Place

Address:	38 Kensington Crescent, Higgovale Cape Town, 8001 South Africa
Phone:	+27 21 424 4744
Fax:	+27 21 424 1810
Website:	www.kensingtonplace.co.za
e-mail:	kplace@mweb.co.za
Located:	Kensington Place is on the slopes of Table Mountain
Style:	contemporary interiors with eclectic African touches throughout
Special features:	a living style lobby with a copper framed fireplace
Rooms:	8 rooms with private terraces
Opening date:	1996
Architecture / Design:	Anton de Kok & Kobus de Vos

Metropole

Address:	38 Long Street
	Cape Town, 8001 South Africa
Phone:	+27 21 424 7247
Fax:	+27 21 424 7248
Website:	www.metropolehotel.co.za
e-mail:	info@metropolehotel.co.za
Located:	right on the city center, close to waterfront
Style:	calm & contemporary with flashes of humor
	& unexpected modern touches
Special features:	M Bar, restaurant Veranda (both open to the public)
Rooms:	29 luxurious rooms (varies gradually in sizes and all are very similar in design)
Opening date:	2004
Architecture / Design:	Kurt Buss
	Francois du Plessis

Jardin D'Ebène

Address:	21 Warren Street, Tamboerskloof Cape Town, 8001 South Africa
Phone:	+27 21 426 1011
Fax:	+27 21 422 2423
Website:	www.jardindebene.co.za
e-mail:	info@jardinebene.co.za
Located:	Jardin D'Ebène is situated in the heart of the City Bowl, right below Table Mountain
Style:	contemporary African style
Special features:	lounge space right next to plunge pool, great atmosphere
Rooms:	4 rooms (names: Zebra, Lion, Elephant, Cheetah
Opening date:	2004
Architecture / Design:	Pascale Lauber & Ulrike Bauschke

Lion's View

Address:	4 First Crescent, Camps Bay Cape Town, 8005 South Africa
Phone:	+27 21 438 1239
Fax:	+27 21 438 0046
Website:	www.lionsview.co.za
e-mail:	info@lionsview.co.za
Located:	5 minutes walk to Camps Bay Beach
Style:	modern style
Special features:	beach and mountain views, heated rim flow swimming pool, spacious lounge, dining room and terraces
Rooms:	main house: 5 bedrooms, 1 with king-size bed, 4 with queen-size beds penthouse: 2 bedrooms, both with queen-sized bed
Opening date:	1999
Architecture / Design:	Greg Wright Architects

Atlanticview Cape Town

Address:	31 Francolin Road, Camps Bay Cape Town, 8005 South Africa
Phone:	+27 21 438 2254
Fax:	+27 21 438 1273
Website:	www.atlanticviewcapetown.com
e-mail:	info@atlanticviewcapetown.com
Located:	top of fashionable Camps Bay alongside green belt nature reserve
Style:	stylish modern with understated elegance
Special features:	gymnasium, massage room, steam facility, 2 infinity pools, breathtaking views from accommodation
Rooms:	5 rooms and 5 suites
Opening date:	2002
Architecture / Design:	Greg Boki, Oswald Nair, Dr. Hammed Khan

Les Cascades de Bantry Bay

Address:	48 de Wet Road, Bantry Bay Cape Town, 8005 South Africa
Phone:	+27 21 434 5209
Fax:	+27 21 439 4206
Website:	www.lescascades.co.za
e-mail:	fontain@mweb.co.za
Located:	in Bantry Bay
Style:	exotic contemporary Middle Eastern style
Special features:	great view from every level & angle of the guest house, every step is a discovery for the eye. 3 pools that face the Atlantic Ocean
Rooms:	6 up, 4 down (more like your own private villa)
Opening date:	1998
Architecture / Design:	Luc & Els Deschouwer

Les Cascades de Bantry

Birkenhead House

Address:	7th Avenue, Voëlklip
	Hermanus, 7200 South Africa
Phone:	+27 28 314 8000
Fax:	+27 28 314 1208
Website:	www.birkenheadhouse.com
e-mail:	info@birkenheadhouse.com
Located:	in Hermanus right on a cliff above the beach
Style:	very unique place with both a contemporary & baroque touch
Special features:	Fullboard including house wine selection, for private events entire hotel can be rented
Rooms:	11 rooms
Opening date:	2003
Architecture / Design:	Phil and Liz Biden, Michael Dall Architects

The Marine

Address:	P.O. Box 9
	Hermanus, 7200 South Africa
Phone:	+27 28 313 1000
Fax:	+27 28 313 0160
Website:	www.marine-hermanus.co.za
e-mail:	hermanus@relaischateaux.com
Located:	perched on top of the cliffs at Hermanus
Style:	a fusion of the original 100 year building and modern innovation
Special features:	spa, conference facilities, gift shop, swimming pool, tidal pool, internet lounge, heli pad
Rooms:	45 individually decorated bedrooms and suites
Opening date:	1998
Architecture / Design:	Liz McGrath

Makalali Game Reserve

Address:	P.O. Box 809 Hoedspruit, 1380 South Africa
Phone:	+27 15 793 1720
Fax:	+27 15 793 1739
Website:	www.makalali.co.za
e-mail:	makalali@icon.co.za
Located:	close to the mighty Drakensberg mountain range, west of the Kruger National Park, in the Gravelotte area of the Limpopo Province of South Africa
Style:	unique and innovative
Special features:	boma, lounge, night sky session, swimming pool all four camps
Rooms:	six spacious suites
Opening date:	1996
Architecture / Design:	Silvio Rech

La Garonga

Address: P.O. Box 737
Hoedspruit, 1380 South Africa
Phone: +27 82 440 3522
Fax: +27 15 318 7902

Website: www.garonga.com
e-mail: safari@garonga.com

Located: the greater Makalali Conservancy situated
west of the Kruger National Park
Style: textured earthy colors and clean lines
Special features: the suite also has an outdoor shower,
as well as a private pool and deck
Rooms: 14 bed camp

Opening date: 1995

Architecture / Design: Trish Marshall

Melrose Arch Hotel

Address: 1 Melrose Square, Melrose Arch
Johannesburg, 2196 South Africa
Phone: +27 11 214 6666
Fax: +27 11 214 6600

Website: www.africanpridehotels.com/melrosearch
e-mail: info@melrosearchhotel.com

Located: 10 km to the Johannesburg city center
Style: humoristic contemporary style
Special features: March Restaurant, library bar, comfortable
veranda, pool bar, sound room
Rooms: 118 rooms

Opening date: 2003

Architecture / Design: Les Harbottle

Ten Bompas

Address:	10 Bompas Road, Dunkeld West Gauteng, Johannesburg, South Africa
Phone:	+27 11 341 0282
Fax:	+27 11 341 0281
Website:	www.tenbompas.com
e-mail:	reservations@mix.co.za
Located:	minutes away from Sandton, Randburg, Hyde Park, Rosebank and Illovo
Style:	contemporary African design
Special features:	guest lounges, a dining room, bar, meeting rooms and conference facilities
Rooms:	10 suites
Opening date:	1995
Architecture / Design:	Luc Zeghers, Designers: Joan Young, Nerina Nicollela, Dee Design, John Crawley, Camign Interior Design, Andre Croucamp, Gill Butler and Anushka Leroni

The Outpost

Address:	Makuleke Region of Kruger National Park, Limpopo Province, South Africa
Phone:	+27 11 341 0282
Fax:	+27 11 341 0281
Website:	www.theoutpost.co.za
e-mail:	reservation@mix.co.za
Located:	situated in the Makuleke Region in the northernmost part of Kruger National Park
Style:	contemporary design expressing simple, clean lines and combining elements of steel and canvas
Special features:	frontage offering a 180 degree views of the Luvuvhu River Valley
Rooms:	12 stand-alone en suite living space
Opening date:	2003
Architecture / Design:	Enrico Daffonchio

Singita Sweni Lodge

Address: P.O. Box 23367, Claremont 7735
Cape Town, South Africa (Reservations)
Phone: +27 21 683 3424
Fax: +27 21 683 3502

Website: www.singita.com
e-mail: singita@singita.co.za

Located: in the Kruger National Park
Style: contemporary African safari style
Special features: intimate lounge and timber-deck dining area overlooking the Sweni River, bar area, library, wine cellar, swimming pool and open boma, health spa, gymnasium, art gallery, wine boutique
Rooms: 6 suites at Singita Sweni Lodge plus 15 suites at neighboring Singita Lebombo Lodge

Opening date: 2003

Architecture / Design: Andrew Makin, Design Workshop
Boyd Ferguson, Cecile and Boyd

Tsala Treetop Lodge

Address:	P.O. Box 454
	Plettenberg Bay, 6600 South Africa
Phone:	+27 44 532 7818
Fax:	+27 44 532 7878
Website:	www.tsala.com
e-mail:	res@hunterhotels.com
Located:	10 km west of Plettenberg Bay
Style:	ethno African rustic
Special features:	exclusive and very private suites
Rooms:	10 treetop suites
Opening date:	2001
Architecture / Design:	Bruce Stafford & Hunter family

Address:	35, Humewood Road
	Port Elizabeth, 6001 South Africa
Phone:	+27 41 582 2245
Fax:	+27 41 582 2246
Website:	www.thewindermere.co.za
e-mail:	info@thewindermere.co.za
Located:	5 minutes from Humewood GC,
	4 km from airport
Style:	contemporary chic with classic comforts
Special features:	a cocktail deck (with magnificent view)
Rooms:	8 luxury suites
Opening date:	2003
Architecture / Design:	Mr. Lochner
	Anne Read

Architectes/Designers, Hotel Page

Architectes/Designers, Hotel Page

Photo Credits

Roland Bauer, Jnane Tamsna (46), Kasbah Agafay (62), Sublime Ailleurs (70),
Dar Ahlam (80), Jumeirah Bab Al Shams (106), Makalali Game Reserve (336),
La Garonga (342), Ten Bompas (358), The Outpost (364), Singita Sweni Lodge (372);
Jran Blais, Heure Bleue Palais (42); **Andreas Burz**, Wolwedans Dune Camp (226),
Mowani Mountain Camp (230), Goche Ganas (240); **Michelle Galindo**, Hemingway House
(246), Kensington Place (254), Metropole (262), Jardin D'Ebène (270), Lion's View (282),
Atlanticview Cape Town (292), Les Cascades de Bantry Bay (302), Birkenhead House
(314), Melrose Arch Hotel (348); **Martin Nicholas Kunz**, Al Maha Desert Resort & Spa
(100), Jumeirah Bab Al Shams (106), Heritage Golf & Spa Resort (130), Voile d'Or Resort
& Spa (138), Legends (148), Hemingway House (246), Kensington Place (254), Metropole
(262), Jardin D'Ebène (270), Lion's View (282), Atlanticview Cape Town (292), Les
Cascades de Bantry Bay (302), Birkenhead House (314), The Marine (328), Makalali Game
Reserve (336), La Garonga (342), Melrose Arch Hotel (348), Ten Bompas (358), Tsala
Treetop Lodge (380); **Ken Niven**, Fundu Lagoon (176); **Heiner Orth**, Hatari (164);
Pere Planells/Tigmi Tagadert, Tigmi (34)

Courtesy: Beit Al Mamlouka (96), Albergo Relais & Châteaux (92), Alfajiri Villas Cover &
(158), Atlanticview Cape Town (292), Benguerra Lodge (204), Conservation Corporation
Africa, Sandibe Safari Lodge (222), Elegant Heritage, Voile d'Or Resort & Spa (138),
Emerson & Green Hotel (172), GHM Hotels, The Chedi Muscat (120), Kasbah du Toubkal
(30), Pamushana (196), Riad des Golfs (20), Riad Farnatchi (54), Shompole (154),
The Windermere (390), Virgin Limited Edition, Kasbah Tamadot (24), Wilderness Safaris,
Kaya Mawa Lodge (184), The River Club (190), Mombo Camp (210), Jao Camp (216)

Special thanks to
Marie-Claude Azzouzi, Joanie Badenhorst, Ulrike Bauschke, Liz and Phil Biden, Anne Bleeker,
Greg Boki, Marko Botes, Stephan Brückner, Scott M. Crouch, Andrea Deininger, Els & Luc
Deschouver, Dale Euston-Brown, Sasha Fernandez, Jörg & Marlies Gabriel, Naomi G. Graham,
Katja Hasselkus, Ian Hunter, Ingo Jacob, Pascale Lauber, Liesl Liebenberg, André Louw,
Meryanna Loum-Martin, Liz McGrath, Paul O'Donnell, Anke Schaffelhuber, Isabell Schreml,
Christoff van Staden, Ingo Stritter, Carmen Thompson

Other Designpocket titles by teNeues:

Each volume:

12.5 x 18.5 cm
400 pages
c. 400 color illustrations